Dangles and Bangles

25 FUNKY ACCESSORIES TO MAKE AND WEAR

Dangles and Bangles

25 FUNKY ACCESSORIES TO MAKE AND WEAR

by Sherri Haab
and Michelle Haab

with illustrations by Barbara Pollak

WATSON-GUPTILL PUBLICATIONS / NEW YORK

Senior Acquisitions Editor: Julie Mazur
Editor: Anne McNamara
Designer: Georgia Rucker
Senior Production Manager: Ellen Greene

Text and photographs copyright © 2005 by Sherri Haab
Illustrations copyright © 2005 by Barbara Pollak

Photography by Dan Haab

First published in 2005 by Watson-Guptill Publications,
a division of VNU Business Media, Inc.,
770 Broadway, New York, N. Y. 10003
www.wgpub.com

Library of Congress Cataloging-in-Publication Data

Haab, Sherri.
Dangles and bangles : 25 funky projects to make and wear / by Sherri and
    Michelle Haab ; with illustrations by Barbara Pollak.
p. cm.
ISBN 0-8230-0064-8 (pb)
1. Dress accessories. 2. Jewelry making. 3. Handicraft. I. Haab, Michelle. II.
    Title.
TT560.H323 2005
745.5—dc22

2004029704

Manufactured in China

First printing, 2005

1 2 3 4 5 6 7 8 / 12 11 10 09 08 07 06 05

Acknowledgments

Thanks to Dan for the beautiful photos

and hours of hard work.

Thank you to Whitney and Rachel

for your great ideas!

Thank you to Darcy for testing

the ideas in this book!

Many thanks to the editorial and design staff

at Watson-Guptill for making

this a great book.

And thanks to Barbara Pollak for

the funky, cool illustrations.

Table of Contents

introduction

Who says you have to spend megabucks just to look good? This book is packed with over twenty-five easy-to-do projects to make your own funky and fashionable accessories. Let your imagination run wild! Make cool charms and oh-so-cute add-ons to decorate your hair, your clothes, your handbags—you name it! Adorn yourself with necklaces, bracelets, and earrings made to match a special outfit, or use pins to add pizzazz to plain jeans. Make charms to personalize a book bag or cell phone, or to dangle from a key chain or two.

The great thing about the projects in this book is that they are made with inexpensive craft supplies and other items that are easy to find and use. Many of the projects use materials that you might already have lying around the house. You can even recycle old stuff to create something entirely new.

Don't worry too much if you can't find exactly what is called for in the materials lists. Instead, think about what you can use as substitutes. Sometimes, your idea may be better than the original—that's when creativity happens. So look in the junk drawer, the button box, or in the garage for stuff you can use to make your own dangles and bangles.

Tools & Techniques

All it takes are a few simple tools and techniques to make the projects in this book. Most of the supplies are easy to find either around the home or at your local arts and crafts store. It's a good idea to stock up on a wide assortment of supplies so that you can get crafty whenever the mood or moment grabs you. All of the projects are easy to make using basic craft techniques like cutting and pasting paper and fabric, or beading and finishing wire and cord. Once you have and know the basics, you'll be free to focus on the fun of designing your own dangles and bangles. Be creative with colors, fabrics, and decorations to make your own, one-of-a-kind styles.

Jewelry Findings

Jewelry findings are the nuts and bolts of jewelrymaking. They're the hardware that holds everything together. You can find jewelry findings in craft stores, bead shops, and catalogs. There are several findings that are used over and over again to make the projects in this book. You will want to keep these common findings on hand so that you can create your favorite dangles and bangles whenever the mood hits you. Here is a list of popular findings and what they are used for:

JUMP RINGS are small metal loops that are used to link pieces together or to attach a charm to a bracelet. Open jump rings by twisting the ends out to each side with pliers. Close the rings by bringing the ends back together.

SPLIT RINGS are like key rings. They can be used in place of jump rings and you don't need to use pliers to work with them. Split rings are great for attaching heavy charms and other pieces that might cause a jump ring to pull apart.

EAR WIRES are available in a variety of styles in craft and bead shops. Designed for using with pierced ears, ear wires have a loop on the bottom that can be attached to a jump ring or directly to your project.

HEAD PINS are short wires with a flat pad or a ball shape at one end. You can add beads onto a head pin and then coil the top to make a loop for hanging.

PIN BACKS are sold in different sizes and styles. They can be glued or sewn to the back of a pin. Some pin backs even come with ready-to-use adhesive strips.

CLASPS are closures used to join the ends of a bracelet or necklace together. Loop-and-toggle, spring ring, and lobster claw are popular types of closures. Use jump rings to attach closures to the ends of your finished bracelets or necklaces.

FINDINGS are the hardware you need to pull your jewelry together. Clockwise from top left: Pin backs, loop-and-toggle clasps, lobster claw clasp, ear wires, silver head pins, brass head pins, eye pins, crimp beads, and jump rings.

Essential Tools

Having the right tools makes a big difference. Just like findings, the same few tools are used again and again to make the projects in this book. Make sure you treat your tools with respect, use them as intended, and follow safety precautions. You don't want to accidentally pinch your fingers with pliers! Using the right cutting tools for the right materials will keep them sharper longer. Here is a list of common tools and how to use them:

A few basic pliers and wire cutters are all you need to make most of the projects in this book. Pictured from top to bottom are wire cutters, round-nose pliers, and needle-nose pliers.

NEEDLE-NOSE PLIERS from the hardware store will work just fine for most tasks. You can open and close jump rings with these common household pliers, and you can even use them to cut wire.

CHAIN-NOSE PLIERS are available in craft and bead shops. These are used to open jump rings, and to crimp or bend wire.

ROUND-NOSE PLIERS are used to form wire loops of different sizes. Use these pliers to make charms that dangle, or use them to form loops on earrings to attach ear wires.

WIRE CUTTERS help to cut wire neatly and up close to your work. You can also use old nail clippers to cut fine wire or plastic-coated craft wire.

PAPER SCISSORS are used to cut paper, cardstock, shrink plastic, and laminate. Small scissors with pointed tips are great for cutting around tight areas.

SEWING SCISSORS should be used only for cutting ribbon, felt, or fabric. Using these scissors to cut paper will eventually dull the blade. (It's a good idea to label your sewing scissors.)

HOLE PUNCHES are available in a variety of shapes and sizes. A standard hole punch is a must for jewelrymaking. Smaller-sized punches are also great to have for making tiny jewelry pieces.

WOODEN SKEWERS, TOOTH-PICKS, AND TWEEZERS make helpful craft tools. Use skewers and toothpicks to apply glue, or wrap wire around them to form loops. Tweezers are great for gluing on small beads and rhinestones.

RULERS are essential for measuring cord and wire, and for drawing straight lines on fabric and paper.

Glues & Adhesives

There is a wide variety of glues and adhesives available for almost any task. Having the right kind of glue can make all the difference in the success of a project. For example, if you use extra-sticky gem glue to glue gems onto fabric, it will be less likely that the gems will pop off of your project. The following is a list of the types of glues used to make the projects in this book:

FABRIC GLUE attaches materials like felt, fabric, rickrack, and ribbon together.

GEM OR JEWEL GLUE is used to glue beads, gems, buttons, and lightweight plastic decorations on materials like fabric and felt.

WHITE CRAFT GLUE is used to glue paper and to attach small items like sequins and glitter. White glue can also be used on fabric and to coat the ends of cord to prevent fraying.

FABRIC HEM SEALANT, such as Fray Check™, dries clear and is used to prevent the ends of cord or cut edges of fabric from fraying.

DECOUPAGE GLUE, such as Mod-Podge®, can be brushed over paper to seal and protect the surface from moisture and wear.

DOUBLE-STICK TAPE AND ADHESIVE SHEETS are sticky on both sides. This allows you to attach surfaces together neatly.

Craft Supplies

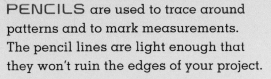

There is a wide assortment of general craft supplies—like ribbons, glitter, pencils, and paint—that can be used for jewelrymaking. All of these materials are easy to find in your local arts and crafts store. Here is a list of your must-haves:

PENCILS are used to trace around patterns and to mark measurements. The pencil lines are light enough that they won't ruin the edges of your project.

PERMANENT MARKERS are great for drawing lines and making marks on plastic.

ACRYLIC PAINTS are good all-purpose craft paints that can be used on most surfaces. Just be sure to wash acrylic paint out of brushes quickly, as it becomes very difficult to remove once it has dried.

PAINTBRUSHES come in lots of shapes and sizes. You should have at least two brushes, one for paint and one for glue. Inexpensive synthetic brushes are great for gluing and for working with acrylic paint. Remember to keep your paint brushes separate from your glue brushes.

GLITTER will add sparkle and shine to your jewelry projects. Scrapbook suppliers and craft stores offer many choices, from silver and gold to lots of bright colors.

PAPER comes in all types and styles. Collage sheets offer tons of images that you can use to decorate accessories. Use decoupage glue to apply collage paper to your project. Other types of paper include tissue papers, metallic papers, and natural fiber papers. Laminate is a clear paper with an adhesive backing that you can layer over your finished project for extra protection.

BUTTONS AND EMBELLISH-MENTS can be found in fabric and craft stores. There are all kinds of fun embellishments that can be used for making jewelry. Metal stamps and charms with words on them come in just the right size for bracelets and necklaces. Scrabble tiles and other game pieces also make great decorations.

Brand names are included on the materials lists of some projects for you to use as a guide when you are looking for supplies. These are my favorites, but you might find other brands that work just as well. There is also a list of craft and jewelrymaking suppliers at the back of the book (see page 95). These suppliers can help you choose and find the materials you're looking for.

Techniques

Y ou don't have to be an expert crafter to make your own dangles and bangles. The projects in this book are not difficult to make, and the step-by-step instructions will tell you everything you need to know to complete your project. Here are some basics to get you started.

Working with Cord & Elastic

Cord and elastic are great materials for jewelrymaking. You can thread beads on them, hang pendants and charms—whatever you like! Cord and elastic come in different weights, colors, and styles. When choosing cord or elastic, be sure it not only has the right look for your project, but also is strong enough to support your decorations.

When working with fabric cord, you'll need to finish the cut ends to prevent them from fraying. To do this, simply apply white glue or a fabric hem sealant, like Fray Check, to the ends of the cord. Let the glue dry and you're all set.

When tying cord or elastic around your wrist or fingers, a **square knot** is a good, secure knot to use. To tie a square knot, hold the ends of the cord in each hand. Cross the right end over the left and then wrap it around, just like when you are tying a bow in your shoelace. Then, repeat the steps, only this time tying the left end over the right end. Pull on the ends to tighten the knot.

A **larks head knot** is a looped knot used to attach objects to cord. To make a larks head knot, make a loop in the center of the cord. Pull the loop through a ring or wrap it around an object. Then bring the ends of the cord through the loop and pull.

Gluing

When working with glue, make sure you cover your work area with newspaper, a paper plate, or an old magazine to protect your work surface. Use a toothpick to apply small dabs or a thin line of glue. Be sure to use the right glue for the material you are using (see Glues & Adhesives, page 14). After applying, leave the glue untouched until it is dry. Keep in mind that fabric glues must be completely dry before a project is wearable.

Working with Jump Rings & Head Pins

There are a few techniques for working with jump rings and head pins that will give your work a professional look.

Do This!

Don't Do This!

Open a jump ring by twisting the ends out to each side with pliers. Close the jump ring in the same manner, bringing the ends back in from the sides.

Don't pull the jump ring open by pulling it apart. This weakens the jump ring and the metal could snap and break.

Head pins are wires used for hanging beads on jewelry chains or earring hooks. To make a head pin dangle, thread your beads on first. Bend the wire at a 90-degree angle, then form a loop with round-nose pliers. Clip off the extra wire or twist the wire around once before clipping with wire cutters.

When working with a head pin, bend the wire at a 90-degree angle, as shown, then use pliers to form the wire into a loop.

Groovy Girl

If you love the free-spirited looks of the '60s and '70s, here are some projects to give your wardrobe a little retro groove. These big bead bracelets, leather cord necklaces, and funky fabric accessories will give your brand-new outfits a cool, laid-back style. As Austin Powers says, "If it looks groovy, wear it man."

Circle Charm Jewelry

These mod, '60s-inspired circle charm earrings, bracelets, and necklaces are the perfect thing for when you're feelin' groovy. Despite their polished look, these jewelry pieces are super easy to make from colorful acrylic circle charms.

ACRYLIC CIRCLE CHARMS come ready to use with one hole for hanging. If you want to link a row of charms, you will need to drill a second hole. A hand drill will actually drill through the acrylic easier than a power drill would. That's because power drills heat the plastic, and cause it to melt and get sticky.

1 To drill a hole in the charm, place the charm on an old phone book or thick catalog. Use a hand drill to drill through the acrylic, using the phone book as a backing. When the drill hits the book, you can crank the handle in reverse to "back out" of the hole.

2 Link the charms together with jump rings. Open and close the jump rings with pliers (see page 17).

HELPFUL HINT: It helps to have an extra helper to hold the charm in place as you drill.

3 To make a bracelet, link charms together until the bracelet fits around your wrist. Use jump rings to add a loop clasp to one end and a toggle to the other end. (You can use another type of clasp if you want.)

4 To make earrings, link a few charms together with jump rings. Don't drill the bottom charm with a second hole. Use jump rings to attach the linked charms to ear wires, and then close the jump rings with pliers.

To make a necklace, link a few charms together with jump rings. Then, hang the linked charms from a chain. You can vary the design by hanging a number of charm dangles on one chain or by using jump rings to attach a couple of single charms along a chain.

Mod Bead Bracelet

Give plain wooden beads a mod makeover with easy-to-do decoupage. Paper napkins, tissue paper, and newspaper are the best choices to decoupage onto beads. You can paint the beads for a splash of color, glue on glitter, or cut out words from magazines to create your own cool styles.

Tissue paper and paper napkins are so thin they glue smoothly over round beads. Overlap the paper pieces to create deeper colors and textures.

24

Tear off small pieces of paper napkin or tissue paper to apply to the beads. Paint small sections of the bead with decoupage glue.

Apply the napkin bits to cover the bead. Continue adding pieces, gluing and overlapping the edges until the bead is covered. (Be careful not to cover the bead holes!)

Roll the end of the paintbrush over the paper to smooth it in place, or use your fingers to smooth the paper (wash your hands if they get too sticky). Let the beads dry.

Seal the beads with a final coat of decoupage glue. Make sure all of the sections are covered with glue. Let the glue dry.

String the beads onto a piece of elastic cord. Tie the cord into a square knot (see page 16). Clip off the excess cord. Put a dab of decoupage glue on the ends of the cord to keep them from fraying.

Butterfly Ankle Bracelets

Summer is the perfect time for wearing dangles on your ankles. Doodle your own butterfly on shrink plastic or trace the template on page 94. You can also trace or draw other shapes to make lots of colorful charms.

MATERIALS

- pre-sanded shrink plastic (Ruff N' Ready by Shrinky Dinks®)
- permanent marker
- pattern or design to trace
- colored pencils (Prisma™ or Crayola™ brand work best)
- scissors
- hole punch
- white glue
- toothpick
- flat-back rhinestones
- glitter
- cord (cut into 12-inch strand)

1 Trace or draw your design with a permanent marker on the sanded side of the shrink plastic. Color in the design with colored pencils.

2 Carefully cut around the outline of the design with scissors. Leave a space at the top of the plastic for a hole. Use your hole punch to punch a hole at the top of the plastic.

3 Shrink your plastic charm, following the directions below. Let cool, then glue rhinestones and glitter onto the colored side of the design. Use a toothpick to apply the glue.

4 Thread the cord through the hole at the top of the charm and then tie the cord around your ankle with a square knot (see page 16). Cut off the excess cord.

SHRINK PLASTIC has been around since the early '70s. It comes in clear, frosted, ivory, brown, and black sheets. When heated, the plastic shrinks to about half of its size and gets thicker and harder. Shrink plastic holds color better if it is sanded first. To save time, you can use pre-sanded sheets, like Ruff N' Ready by Shrinky Dinks.

All you need is a regular oven to bake shrink art. Place the pieces on a glass baking sheet or on a clean sheet of paper. Pre-heat the oven to 275-325 degrees. Note: Some brands and types of plastic differ in baking temperature; refer to the manufacturer's guidelines for the right baking temperature for the plastic you are using. The plastic pieces usually only take a few minutes to shrink. The plastic will curl up while heating and then flatten back out after shrinking. If a piece sticks to itself you can remove it from the oven, let it cool down, and then try to un-stick it. Then return the piece to the oven and re-heat it. BE CAREFUL NOT TO BURN YOUR FINGERS! IT'S A GOOD IDEA TO TRY A FEW SAMPLE PIECES BEFORE YOU HEAT AND SHRINK YOUR PROJECT. USE A POT HOLDER TO PROTECT YOUR HANDS AND HAVE AN ADULT AROUND TO HELP YOU OUT.

These clear bauble pendants are the perfect accessories for hippy-style clothing. The baubles are made from flat-backed marbles, which can be easily found in floral and craft stores.

MATERIALS

- clear flat-backed marbles
- paper images (The Vintage Workshop)
- decoupage glue
- paintbrush (for glue)
- air-dry clay (Makin's Clay™)
- plastic-coated wire
- wire cutters or nail clippers
- jump rings
- necklace chain
- pliers

1 Slide a marble over the paper images to find a picture that fits nicely behind the glass. Cut the image out roughly, being sure to leave extra paper outside the outline.

2 Brush decoupage glue on the flat side of the marble and press the marble on top of the image. Smooth the back of the paper to remove any air bubbles.

3 Trim the excess paper away with scissors. Press the back of the image again to make sure the paper is adhered.

4 Coat the back, paper-covered side of the bauble with glue. Let the glue dry.

5 Roll a marble-sized ball of clay in your hands and flatten it into a round pad. Place the clear marble face-up into the center of the clay, as shown. Mold the edges of the clay around the marble.

6 Cut a small piece of wire and bend it in half to make a hook. Bend the wire ends out a bit to give the hook extra hold. Press the hook into the top of the clay, pushing in as deep as you can. Let dry overnight. Use pliers to add a jump ring and hang the bauble from a chain.

When you place an image behind a clear, flat-backed marble it is magnified with a cool 3-D effect. Slide the marbles over pictures in magazines, newspapers, and wrapping papers to find good images for making baubles.

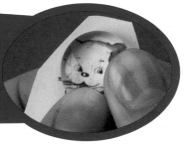

Leather Cord Jewelry

Leather cord accessories go just right with casual, laid-back styles. Decorated with colorful, large plastic beads, these jewelry pieces are held in place with simple knots that slide open and close with ease.

MATERIALS

- 24- to 36-inch piece of 2mm round leather cord
- large plastic beads (with holes large enough to string on cord)
- scissors
- large donut-shaped bead (for pendant)
- tape measure
- pencil

Beaded Leather Bracelet

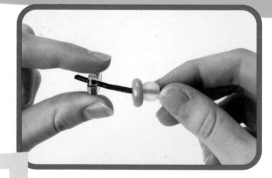

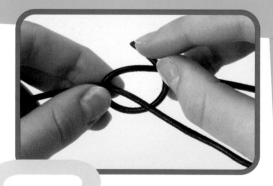

1 Wrap the tape measure around the widest part of your hand and add about 6 to 10 inches (you will need this extra cord for tying the knots). Cut the leather cord to this measurement. Thread large plastic beads onto the leather cord.

2 Tie one end of the cord around the other end. Hint: One end remains straight like a rod while the other end is tied around it once and then looped through itself, as shown.

Pull the knot to tighten. Slip the cord over your hand. Adjust the cord so that the bracelet fits comfortably around your wrist. Make a small pencil mark where the second knot should be tied.

Carefully remove the bracelet. Tie a knot at the pencil mark, this time using the other end of the cord. (There should be a knot around each cord end, as shown.) Put the bracelet on, and then slide and tighten the knots as needed for a comfortable fit.

Leather Cord Necklace with Pendant

With the tape measure, measure around your head and then add about 6 to 10 inches extra for tying knots. Use a larks head knot to attach the donut bead to the cord. To make a larks head knot, fold the cord in half and put the looped center of the cord through the bead hole, as shown.

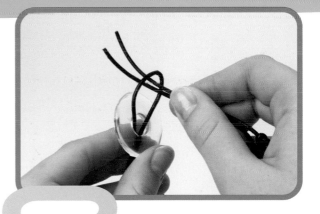

Bring the ends of the cord through the loop and pull. Hold the cord ends together and add on a few more beads, resting the beads on top of the donut bead. Finish the necklace as you did for the bracelet (see steps 2 through 4, above), adjusting the knots as needed.

'60s fabric belt

Hip-hugger jeans topped with soft fabric belts were all the rage in the '60s. This fabric belt is made by "finger crocheting" a chain stitch. Complete the retro look with a classic floral print, or choose a fabric that matches a favorite top or T-shirt.

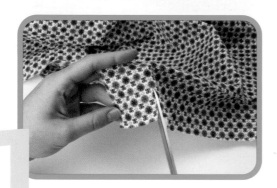

1

To link the strips, cut a slit at each end of each strip about ½ inch from the end (the slit should be cut about ½ inch long and cut in the same direction as the length of the strip). Pull one strip through the slit of another strip to join them. To secure the link, pull the tail end of the strip you just pulled through, back through its own slit and tug tightly.

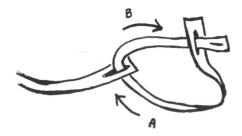

2. Make a slip knot to attach the joined strips to the buckle. To start, pull one end of the strip through the buckle, leaving a 6-inch tail of fabric. Wrap the long end around the tail, as shown, to make a loop. Poke the long end through the center of the loop, following the arrows in the photo.

3. This photo shows the new loop you just made. Don't pull the strip all of the way through. This is your first slip knot. You will use the open loop of this knot to form your next stitch. The chain stitch is simply a series of slip knots.

4. Continue making a chain, taking the long working end and pulling a new loop through the previous loop. Pull the knots as you go, keeping the loops nice and even.

5. Keep making loops in a chain until you can fit the belt around your waist. To complete the chain, pull the long working end through the last loop, this time pulling the end all the way through.

6. To finish, go back to the start and weave the loose end into the chain stitches to hide.

Instead of finger crocheting, you can just braid three strips of fabric together to make a belt. Or, simply tie strips of fabric or a scarf onto a belt loop for an instant fashion accessory. Look for buckle findings in the notions section of your local sewing or crafts store.

flower power pins

Big blooms are showing up on everything these days. They can be used to hold together a wrap or button-up top, or attach them to a T-shirt, choker, or even a belt for a sassy splash of color and style.

MATERIALS

- 12-inch piece of printed cotton fabric
- 6 x 12-inch sheet double-sided adhesive (PEELnSTICK™ by Therm O Web)
- small piece of felt (about 2-inch square)
- pencil
- tracing paper
- paper scissors
- sewing scissors
- needle and thread
- gem or jewel glue
- button, pom-pom, or large bead (for flower center)
- pin-back finding

Scraps of printed cotton fabrics make great flower pins. Adhesive sheets allow you to make neat, crisp petals without using a sewing machine. If you want to make a flower for your hair, just glue a hair clip to the back instead of a pin-back finding.

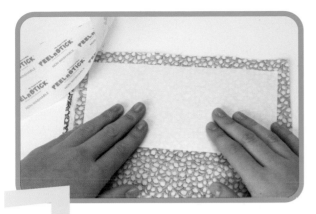

Remove the protective paper from one side of the double-sided adhesive. Press the sticky side onto the wrong side (or the back side) of the fabric, covering half of the fabric. Remove the remaining protective paper from the adhesive.

Fold the other half of the fabric over and press it onto the adhesive. Smooth the entire surface to make sure that the fabric layers are adhered.

Trace either the oval- or round-shaped petal pattern on page 94 onto tracing paper and cut out to make a template. With your pencil, trace around the template onto the fabric to make either six oval or five round petals.

Cut out the fabric petals with sewing scissors. Trace the pattern on page 94 for the flower back onto paper and cut out to make a template. Trace the template and transfer the pattern markings onto the felt.

Thread the needle, then match and knot the ends to double the thread. Stitch up through the felt circle at the first pattern mark.

Fold one of the petals in half, pinching the petal at the bottom. Stitch through the bottom of the pinched petal, sewing through both fabric layers.

Slide the petal over the outer edge of the felt circle, as shown. Pull the thread tightly to hold the petal shape. Stitch down through the felt, close to the petal.

Come back up through the felt and slide another petal in place, next to the first. Stitch the second petal in place in the same manner as you did in step 7. Pull the thread tightly to keep the petals folded.

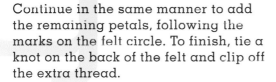

Continue in the same manner to add the remaining petals, following the marks on the felt circle. To finish, tie a knot on the back of the felt and clip off the extra thread.

Use gem glue to attach a button to the center of the flower. (Adjust the petals as needed before gluing.) Turn the flower over and glue on a pin-back finding. Let the glue dry. You can also sew the pin-back on for extra hold.

Out & About

When you're getting set to go out with your friends, the first things you think to bring along are the essentials—your cell phone, purse, and house keys. Fashion-smart girls make these must-haves much more by dressing them up with playful charms and accessories. Whether you're set to cruise the mall or hit your favorite downtown destinations, these easy-to-do projects will make you a stylish standout.

Robot Key Chains

These fun and funky robot key chains can double as charms for cell phones, handbags, and belt loops. The robot parts can be purchased in stores, or look around your home for odds and ends to use. The robot body can be made out of a paper clip, a button, or a can pop-top.

MATERIALS

- 36-inch length of plastic-coated wire
- plastic pony bead
- large wooden bead
- star washer
- plastic paper clip (Plastiklips™ by Baumgarten)
- metal springs (from the hardware store or spiral ring bindings from copy center)
- clear plastic vinyl tubing, 1/4 to 3/8 inch diameter (cut into 1 1/4- to 1 1/2-inch lengths)
- 4 plastic beads (for hands and feet)
- wire cutters or nail clippers
- jump ring
- key chain

Most of the materials needed to make robot charms can be found in large department stores. Look for nuts, washers, and springs in the hardware section, plastic tubing in the plumbing section, and paper clips among the school and office supplies. Beads and plastic-coated wires can be found wherever craft supplies are sold.

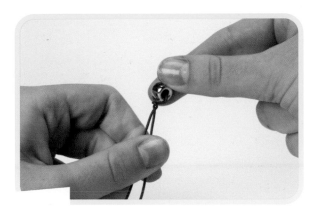

Collect all of the materials you need before beginning the project. Slide the plastic pony bead to the center of the wire. Twist the wire ends around a few times to secure the bead in place.

For the robot head, slide the large wooden bead over both wire ends and pull it all of the way up to the pony bead.

For the robot neck, slide a star washer over both wire ends and pull it all of the way up to the wooden bead.

At the bottom of the robot neck, pull the two wire ends out in opposite directions. Attach a wire end to each side of the office clip by wrapping the wire around the outer part of the clip a few times, as shown.

Starting on one side, thread a piece of clear tubing, a spring, or both over the wire to form an arm. Hint: Make your own wire coils by wrapping plastic-coated wire around a large needle, wooden skewer, or similar object.

Add a bead for the hand (a star-shaped bead like the one shown will look very handlike). Loop the wire over the bead and back through the arm tube, and then pull the wire tight. Repeat steps 5 and 6 to complete the other arm.

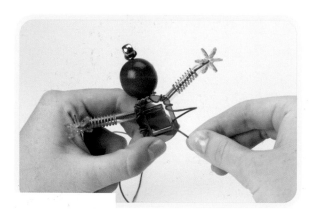

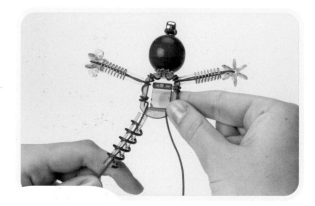

Continue wrapping the wire ends down the sides of the clip, as shown, until you reach the bottom of the clip.

Thread one of the wires through a tube and spring to form one of the robot legs.

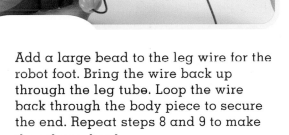 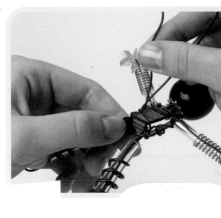

Add a large bead to the leg wire for the robot foot. Bring the wire back up through the leg tube. Loop the wire back through the body piece to secure the end. Repeat steps 8 and 9 to make the other robot leg.

Finish by twisting the ends of the wires together on the back of the body. Clip off the excess wire. Attach the robot to a key chain with a large jump ring.

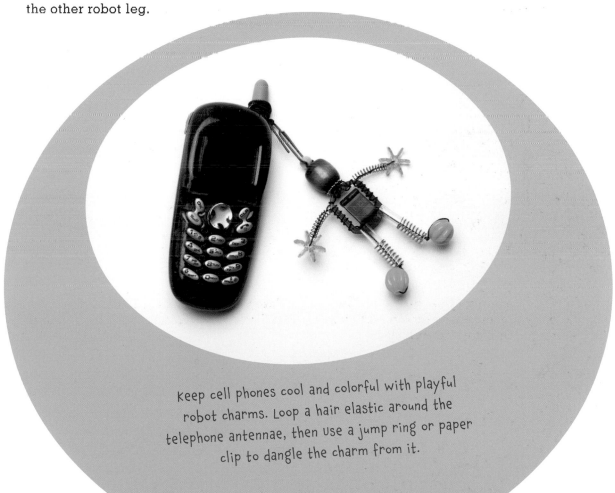

Keep cell phones cool and colorful with playful robot charms. Loop a hair elastic around the telephone antennae, then use a jump ring or paper clip to dangle the charm from it.

Dial in to the newest trend—sweet and sassy cell phone charms. Little plastic party toys, like the ones you get from gumball machines, make great cell-phone dangles. Look for small plastic toys or party favors that have an opening on top to loop the elastic through for hanging.

MATERIALS

- gumball machine toys or party favors
- covered hair elastics or rubber bands

Attach the elastic onto the toy with a larks head knot (see page 16). Pull a loop of elastic through a hole or opening on the top of the toy. Pull one end of the elastic through the loop. Pull tight to secure the elastic in place. Use a larks head knot to attach the toy to the antennae of your cell phone or attach toys to a belt loop, as shown.

44

Felt Flower Pins

Start with a simple wool cap, add a bunch of colorful flowers, and—voilà!—you've got a hip head-warmer. The felt flowers are attached to pin-back findings, so they can be used to decorate hats, sweaters, bags, and more. Make a bunch of flower pins to add a touch of springtime to all your cool-weather gear.

MATERIALS

- 9 × 12-inch felt square
- needle and thread
- gem glue
- pin-back finding
- sewing scissors

For a different look, draw a flower pattern on paper and cut out to make a template. Trace the template two or three times on felt, then cut out and layer the felt pieces. Top the flower with a small bud. You can also make flowers by gathering and stitching strips of felt and surrounding them with petals. To finish, frame your bouquet with some green felt leaves.

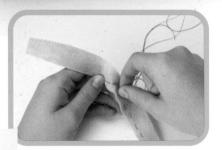

Cut two or three ¾-inch-wide strips from the long edge of the felt. (Don't worry if the strips are a bit uneven.) Cut out a small circle for the flower back (see pattern on page 94). Sew along the bottom of one of the strips with a long running stitch (that is, a row of long stitches going in and out of the fabric).

Pull the thread to lightly gather the strip (think of a curtain on a rod). Don't pull too tight or the felt will bunch up too much. The gathered felt should start to curve into a circle shape, as shown. Knot the thread and clip off the excess. Follow steps 1 and 2 to gather the other strips.

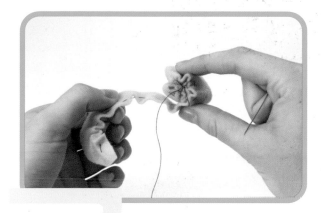

To form the flower, roll one of the strips into a coil. Sew the gathered and rolled edge of the strip with a whipped stitch. To whip-stitch, stitch through one layer, bring the thread over the edge of the fabric, and then stitch through the next layer. Continue coiling and stitching, adding strips as you go until the flower reaches the desired fullness. Knot and clip the thread.

Use gem glue to glue a circle of felt to the center back of the flower, covering the stitching. Let the glue dry. To finish, glue a pin-back finding to the back of the felt circle. Pin the flower on your cap, coat lapel, or anywhere else you desire. If you want to make a flower to wear in your hair, attach a barrette instead of a pin back (see illustration above).

Duct Tape Coin Purses

MATERIALS

- roll of red duct tape, 2 inches wide
- roll of silver duct tape, 2 inches wide
- scissors
- sheet of paper
- permanent marker
- hole punch
- key chain

These little purses are just the right size for carrying movie tickets or a few dollars. Duct tape is available in a variety of colors and widths. Check out your local hardware or department store or look online for a variety of duct tape choices.

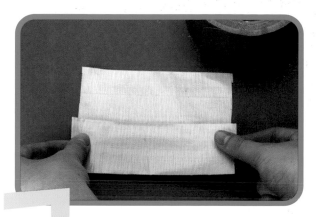

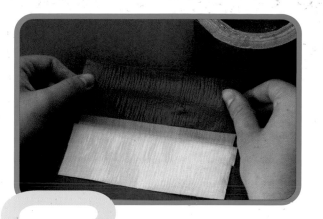

Cut three 8-inch-long strips of tape. With the sticky sides up, attach the strips to each other to make a sheet of tape. Overlap each strip of tape slightly over the last to make the sheet.

Cut three more 8-inch strips of tape. Cover the sticky side of the sheet of tape with the new strips of tape, sticky sides together. Overlap each strip of tape slightly over the last to cover the sheet. Follow steps 1 and 2 to make a second sheet of tape.

Trace the pattern on page 94 onto paper and cut out to make a template. Trace around the template on both sheets of tape with a permanent marker. Cut out the two heart shapes.

Start with one of the hearts. Cut two thin strips of tape (about ¼ inch wide) to cover the rounded curves on top of the heart. Wrap the tape over the top of the curves, starting in the "dip" of the hearts as shown. Make sure the tape is centered along the edge.

5 Trim the ends of the tape so that the tape only covers the curved top sections of the heart, as shown. Repeat the steps to cover the top of the curves of the second heart.

6 Pinch the tape along the top of the curves so that the tape covers the top edges. Repeat to cover the edges of the second heart.

7 Layer the two hearts together, matching the edges. Cut another thin piece of tape and place it along the straight edge on one side of the hearts, as shown. Pinch the tape over the edge to hold the two layers together. Trim off the excess tape at the bottom of the heart. Repeat on the other side, taping the sides together.

8 Open up the top of the heart purse and punch a hole through one layer on one side. Punch through the hole you made a second time to punch a matching hole in the other layer.

Decorate the purse with skinny strips of silver tape or with other cut shapes of tape if you desire. Attach the purse to a key chain to hang from your handbag or backpack.

Rectangle Coin Purses

Follow steps 1 through 2 to make two sheets of silver duct tape. Cut both sheets to measure 3½ inches wide by 3 inches tall. Layer the rectangles together, matching the edges. Cut three thin pieces of tape. Tape the bottom and sides of the rectangle together to form the purse. Decorate as desired. Follow steps 8 and 9 to finish the coin purse.

Fashion Victim Key Chains

This is your chance to be a fashion model...well, at least to dress your picture like one! Look through your favorite magazines for slamming outfits you can cut out and glue together to make funky paper-doll key chains of you and your friends.

MATERIALS

- photos (of yourself and your friends)
- fashion magazines (to cut up)
- glue stick
- cardstock or heavy paper
- clear laminating film
- gem or jewel glue
- scissors
- hole punch
- pliers
- jump ring
- key chain
- sequins, glitter, small beads, and trim

Don't worry about whether the sizes of all the pieces match—its fun to make the dolls a little offbeat by mixing up or exaggerating sizes.

1 Cut out a nice headshot of you or one of your friends. Cut out clothing pieces and accessories from fashion magazines. Layer and glue the head and fashion pieces onto cardstock using a glue stick.

2. Cut a strip of clear laminate large enough to cover the doll. Peel the protective paper off the laminate. Press the laminate, sticky side down, over the doll. Use another piece of laminate to cover the back of the doll. Smooth the laminate on both sides with your hands.

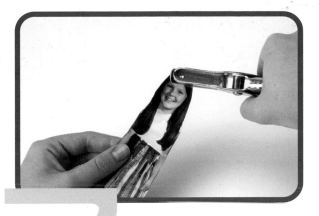

3. Cut out the doll. Punch a hole at the top of the doll for hanging.

4. Use gem glue to decorate the doll with sequins, beads, or trim. Spread a thin layer of glue over selected areas and sprinkle glitter onto the glue. Shake off the excess. Lay the doll flat and let the glue dry overnight.

5. Use pliers to attach the finished doll to a key chain with a large jump ring (see page 17).

Photo Key Chain Belt

Wear your favorite photos around your waist for the ultimate, all-about-you accessory. To make the belt, you will need to first reduce the photos on a copier or computer to fit in the little picture windows. In addition to photos, you can make your belt from words and pictures cut out from magazines.

MATERIALS

- multi pack of plastic key chains with picture inserts (you will need about 12-14 key chains to make one belt)
- plastic clip-style key chain (for clasp)
- pictures or photos
- pencil
- scissors

PLASTIC KEY CHAINS are sold in inexpensive multi packs. Bring out a bunch of key chains and photos for a super slumber party craft.

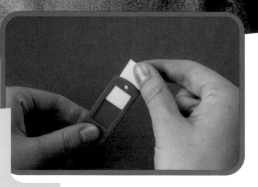

Reduce your photos on a copier or computer to fit inside the key chain windows. Print the photos in color or in black and white on regular copy paper. Remove the split ring at the top of the key chain and set it aside. Remove the cardboard and plastic insert from the key chain.

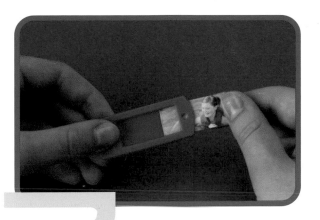

Use one of the inserts as a pattern to trace around the pictures. Cut the first picture out, following the traced lines.

Slip the cut picture through the protective plastic insert into the key chain. Repeat to add photos into each key chain being used to make the belt.

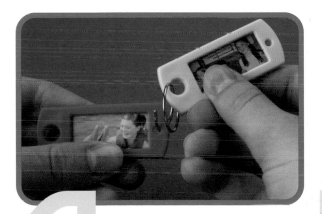

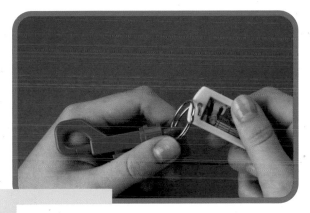

Link the picture key chains together with the split rings that you removed and set aside in step 1. Continue linking the key chains until the belt is the desired length. (The belt can wrap once or twice around your waist.)

When the belt has reached the desired length, add a plastic clip key chain to one end and a split ring to the other end. Wrap the belt around your waist, and then clip the key chain into the split ring to fasten the belt in place.

Gettin' Glam

Want to stand out in the crowd? Think glittery earrings, pretty ribbons, and flowery hair pins. Whether you're aiming for a deliciously simple daytime look or a head-turning party-night style, this chapter is for you. See how with just some scissors and glue, beads and baubles, you can make loads of oh-so-lovely jewelry pieces and hair accessories. With a few simple steps even a plain fishing swivel can be turned into a thing of beauty!

Cherry Jewelry

In the '30s and '40s cherry jewelry was very popular. Back then, it was made out of a plastic called Bakelite. Now you can make your own vintage-styled cherry jewelry using glass or plastic beads and plastic-coated wire. Follow the steps to make a cherry bracelet with matching earrings and a necklace for a bright and cheerful jewelry set with retro flair.

Silver chain is the best choice to accent the bright red "cherries." Look for inexpensive chain bracelets in jewelry, gift, and department stores, or purchase them online.

With your clippers, snip off about 3 inches of wire. Slide a green leaf bead onto the center of the wire.

Loop the wire at the bottom of the leaf bead. Twist one of the wires around the other, as shown. Don't twist too tight—you want to leave a round loop of wire with the leaf in the center.

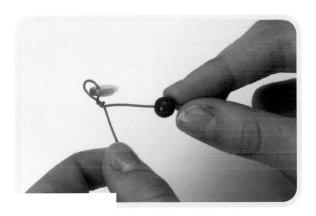

Slide a round bead onto the end of each wire. If you want the stems to be a bit shorter, use your clippers to trim the wire ends.

Use pliers or tweezers to bend the ends of each wire over, as shown. Then crimp or "squish" the wire ends with the pliers. (This will keep the beads from sliding off of the wires.) This completes one "cherry cluster" for the bracelet. Repeat steps 1 through 4 to make a total of seven cherry clusters.

Arrange the clusters evenly along the chain bracelet. Attach the finished cherry clusters to the chain with jump rings. Open the jump rings with pliers and close after attaching to the chain.

Cherry Earrings

Follow steps 1 through 4 to make two cherry clusters. Use jump rings to attach the finished clusters to earring hooks. Open the jump rings with pliers and close after attaching to the hooks.

Cherry Necklace

Follow steps 1 through 4 to make one cherry cluster. (If you want, you can use larger round beads to make a pendant.) Use a jump ring to hang the finished cluster to a chain or ribbon. Open the jump ring with pliers and close after attaching to the chain.

Button Bracelets

MATERIALS
- 1/4-inch wide ribbon, about 14-inch length
- scissors
- 8–10 flat-back buttons (depending on button size)
- pencil
- gem or jewel glue
- needle and thread

A button box is a great source for jewelry ideas. Make bracelets using shades of the same color for both the ribbon and buttons, or for a more striking look, alternate colors such as black and white or pink and black. You can even use metal or jeweled buttons to make the bracelets extra fancy.

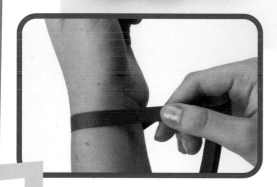

1 Wrap the center of the ribbon around your wrist, leaving extra ribbon on each end for the ties. Mark the size of your wrist on the ribbon with a pencil.

2 Use gem or jewel glue to tack the buttons in a row along the ribbon. Let the glue dry overnight. For extra hold, thread a sewing needle and, starting from the back of the ribbon, sew the buttons in place. Tie the bracelet to your wrist with a bow. Trim off the excess ribbon if needed.

Ribbon Jewelry

Small pieces of ribbon can be used to make stylish bracelets and necklaces. You can simply tie the ribbon around your wrist or add clasps to the ends for a more finished look.

MATERIALS

- ribbon
- scissors
- belt clips
- 2 small jump rings
- clasp and ring or loop and toggle clasp
- pliers
- gem or fabric glue
- buttons, mini stick-on Scrabble tiles (by EK Success), or pendant

BELT CLIPS are bar-shaped clips with teeth along one side. They are usually found in the scrapbook section of the craft store. Choose clips that match the width of your ribbon. Use pliers to crimp the clips over the ends of the ribbon to secure them in place.

Scrabble Bracelet with Belt Clips

1 Cut a piece of ribbon to fit around your wrist. Use pliers to squeeze a belt clip over the ribbon at each end. Squeeze one side of the clip and then move the pliers to the other side until the teeth on the clip are grasping the ribbon.

2 Apply stick-on Scrabble tiles to the ribbon to spell a name or word. (Stick-on tiles are available in the scrapbook section of craft stores.) Or, use gem glue to apply other decorations.

3 Attach small jump rings and a clasp to the clips on the ends. Use pliers to close the jump rings.

Button Bracelet with Clasp

1 Slide a button with a shank (loop on the back) onto the ribbon before adding the belt clips.

2 Attach large jump rings to each clasp. Thread the ribbon ends through the jump rings. Fold the ribbon over and glue with fabric or gem glue. Let dry overnight.

Ribbon Necklace with Pendant

Instead of using a clasp, you can simply tie the ends of the ribbon into a bow. Cut the ribbon to the desired necklace length plus an extra 16 inches for a generous bow. Apply a small amount of white craft glue or hem sealant (see page 14) to the cut ends of the ribbon to prevent the fabric from fraying. Hang a purchased pendant or charm from the ribbon, then tie the ribbon in a big bow.

Bauble and Sequin Earrings

Who said you had to spend big bucks to look fabulous? These sparkly earrings are made with inexpensive plastic beads and sequins from the craft store. Combine the two to make earrings that are oh-so-fun and funky. They are perfect to wear out to a dance or to a party.

MATERIALS
- 2 plastic beads
- 4 seed beads
- assorted sequins
- 2 head pins
- 2 earring wires
- round-nose pliers or wooden skewer
- wire cutters or nail clippers

NOTE: We used two round plastic beads and four seed beads to make the sample pair of earrings, but you can use any combination of beads you like. Add more beads to make longer dangles, or top round beads with flower-shaped beads for a dressy look.

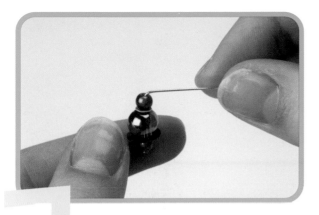

Thread beads and sequins onto a head pin. (For the sample project, we threaded a seed bead on first, followed by a sequin and a larger bead. Finish with another sequin and a seed bead.) At the bottom of the last bead, bend the top of the head pin over into a 90-degree angle.

With your pliers, loop the bent wire back over at the top of the dangle. Wrap the wire around the round-nose pliers or a wooden skewer to make a nice loop.

Add an earring wire to the wire loop, as shown.

Wrap the wire around the base of the loop once to secure the dangle. Clip off the excess wire with wire cutters. Repeat steps 1 through 4 to make a matching earring to complete the pair.

Sequin Bracelets

When you want to razzle and dazzle 'em, sequins are definitely the way to go. Nothing dresses up a simple dress or top more than a swirl of sparkly sequins around your wrist. Combine sequins of different shapes, colors, and sizes to make a trio of glittery bracelets to wear together or separately.

MATERIALS

- assorted sequins
- 24-gauge wire
- wire cutters or nail clippers
- 1 large seed bead, size 6/0 ("E bead")

Sequins are easy to find in craft, sewing, and variety stores. They are available in a wide variety of shapes and colors. The best part is that for a very low cost you can get a large package holding hundreds of sequins. You'll be able to make enough bracelets for all of your friends and loved ones combined!

NOTE: This size of seed bead is also referred to as an "E bead." While larger than most seed beads, E beads are still called seed beads because of their shape and cut.

Cut off about 36 inches of wire. Choose a large sequin that will be used for the "button clasp" at the end of the bracelet. Bend the wire in the middle and make a loop that is big enough for the large sequin to pass through, but not so big that the sequin will slide easily out. Twist the wires a few times at the base of the loop. You will now have a loop with two wire ends.

Thread your first sequin onto one of the wires. Then pass the other wire through the sequin in the opposite direction.

Slide the sequin close to the loop, being careful not to twist the wires. The sequin should lie flat with the wires passing over the surface.

Add the next sequin as you did in steps 1 through 3. Slide the second sequin next to the first. Turn the sequin around twice to twist the wires between the sequins. This will keep them neatly spaced and separated.

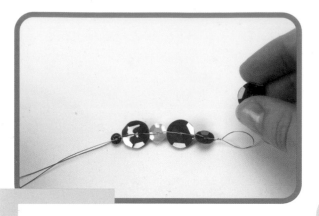

5 Continue adding sequins. For an interesting pattern, mix large and small sequins of different colors along the wires. Measure the bracelet around your wrist as you work.

6 As soon as you have enough sequins threaded on the wires to make a bracelet, add your large "button" sequin on the end. This time pass both ends of the wire through the sequin at the same time going in the same direction. Add the large seed bead on next, sliding the bead next to the sequin.

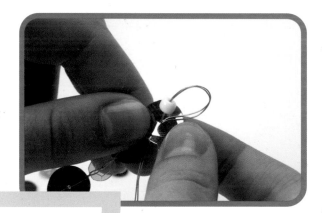

7 Bring both ends of the wires back through the large sequin, skipping over the bead. The bead will act as a "stop," preventing the wire from slipping back through the sequin.

8 Twist the wire ends around the wires directly under the large sequin several times to secure the sequins in place. Clip off the excess wire with wire cutters or nail clippers to finish the bracelet.

Fishing Swivel Bracelet

MATERIALS

- fishing swivels
- seed beads

Fishing swivels make instant jewelry—all you need are beads and swivels to make a bracelet. Jewelrymaking with swivels is a great activity for camping or long car trips. For an extra touch, add pretty charms to dangle from the bracelet.

FISHING SWIVELS are small metal items used to keep fishing lines from tangling (they are also sometimes used on kite strings for the same reason). Swivels come in different sizes and can be found wherever fishing supplies are sold. Keep in mind that smaller swivels are easier to open than larger ones.

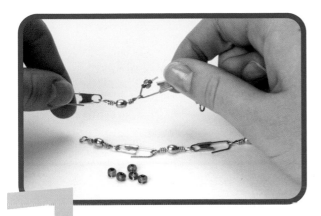

1 First open up the wires on all of the swivels. (You will need about eight swivels to complete a bracelet.) Link the swivels together before adding the beads. Don't close the wires yet! Thread on a few small seed beads to the open wires.

2 Pinch the open hooks closed. If they are stiff, you can use pliers to close them, or ask someone with strong thumbs to close the wires for you.

3 Keep adding links until the swivel chain fits around your wrist. Link the last open wire to the first to close the bracelet around your wrist.

Glittery Hair Flowers

Add sparkle to ordinary fabric flowers to create super-stylish hair accessories just right for a night out with friends. Look in craft and home decorating stores for fabric flowers in a wide selection of fabrics, shapes, and sizes. Choose flowers to match your favorite outfits or combine flowers to create colorful "bouquets."

MATERIALS

- fabric flowers
- white glue (Sobo®)
- adhesive-backed fabric (Delta FabriCraft™ Peel 'n' Stick)
- glitter
- rhinestones
- hair clips, bobby pins, or hair elastics
- sewing scissors
- old scissors (optional, for cutting stems)
- paintbrush (for gluing)

If you don't have adhesive-backed fabric, you can apply white glue to a strip of plain fabric and glue the strip in place. The fabric helps to provide a flexible surface area for gluing the hair clip to the flower.

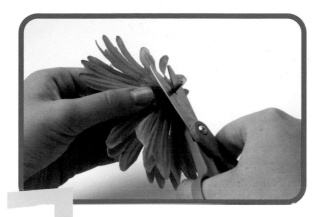

Pull the flowers off of the stems, or clip the stems off with an old pair of scissors.

Some flowers have a bulky plastic center that holds the petals together. If so, remove the plastic center.

Remove any plastic pieces between the petals by gently pulling each petal apart. Reassemble the petals by gluing them together. Let the glue dry.

Brush the center of the flower with white glue. Sprinkle glitter over the wet glue. Shake off the excess.

5 Glue rhinestones onto the petals. Add a drop of white glue at the tip of a petal, and then position a rhinestone in place. Repeat for each petal. Let the glue dry overnight.

6 To attach the flower to a hair clip, cut a small strip from a roll of adhesive-backed fabric. Remove the protective backing.

7 Place the fabric strip adhesive-side-down and centered over the inside of the hair clip, as shown.

8 Press the adhesive strip onto the back of the flower, pressing firmly to adhere the strip to the flower fabric. Let the glue dry completely before wearing the clip.

If you want to attach a bobby pin to a lily flower, slide the bobby pin straight down over the petals and push down into the center of the flower (you may have to remove the plastic base to reveal a hole in the bottom of the flower).

To attach a hair elastic to a flower, follow steps 6 through 7, but attach the strip of adhesive-backed fabric to a hair elastic instead of a clip. Press the adhesive-backed strip over the elastic and onto the flower.

Fun Lovin'

Girls just wanna have fun—and who can blame them?! Fun-loving girls go for quirky styles, unusual materials, and offbeat looks. To them, comic strips are the finest of art, every math problem has a fashion solution, and rings are for wearing on fingers AND toes. If any of this sounds familiar, then this is the chapter for you. On the following pages you'll find projects that are a blast to make and hip to wear.

Junk Drawer Charm Bracelets

Go on a treasure hunt for small objects you can hang from a bracelet. Everyday objects like safety pins, game pieces, beads, and buttons can make funky and colorful charms. Look for items that have an opening to connect with a jump ring. Add beads or jewelry charms to make a design that is truly one of a kind.

MATERIALS

- chain bracelet
- jump rings (1 for each charm)
- head pins
- small found objects (plastic capsule toys, safety pins, beads, buttons, game pieces, or anything small you can hang)
- round-nose pliers
- wire clippers or nail cutters

Collect an assortment of charms to hang from your bracelet. Before you start jewelrymaking, first arrange the charms in a pleasing order along the chain. This will help you to see how far to space them apart and what objects look good next to each other.

78

1 Charms with openings can be attached to the chain with a jump ring. First, open the jump ring with your pliers. Thread the opened jump ring through the opening in the charm. Then, attach the jump ring to the chain and close the ring with your pliers.

2 Beads need a head pin before they can be attached to a jump ring. You can find interesting beads, like the dice bead in the photo above, to hang from your bracelet. Thread the head pin through the bead.

3 Bend the head pin wire over in a 90-degree angle. Loop the wire at the top of the object with round-nose pliers. (If you don't have pliers, you can wrap the wire around a wooden skewer to make a loop.)

4 Wrap the end of the head pin wire around the base of the loop a few times to secure the loop in place.

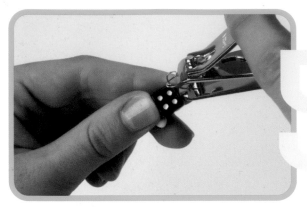

Clip off the excess wire with wire cutters or old fingernail clippers. Continue adding pieces until you have covered the length of the chain.

Treasure Capsule Charms

These capsule charms are a pirate's prize in themselves. Slip a secret note inside a tiny bottle, or make your own treasure trove inside a mini glass. Add a little lock and key for an air of mystery, then hang the charms from your book bag or purse.

MATERIALS

- small corked bottles or clear candy dispensers
- sheet of paper (for funnel)
- tape
- tiny objects (seashells, beads, miniature figures, or bits of paper)
- sand or glitter (to fill the bottom of the bottle)
- white glue
- cord or elastic (for hanging)

1 Use a funnel to fill the bottles with sand. To make a funnel, roll a small square of paper into a cone shape and tape the edge to finish. Place the tip of the funnel inside the bottle, then pour the sand through the funnel.

2 Fill the bottle with small seashells, beads, or other small objects. (Either collect your own tiny seashells or purchase bags of mini shells from a craft store.)

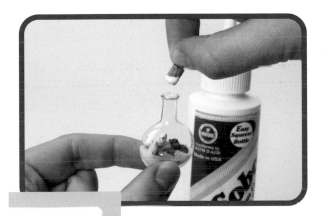

3 Fill the bottle until it is about one third of the way full, as shown. Glue the cork into place with white glue. Note: Don't tip the bottle as the glue dries or the sand will stick to the glue.

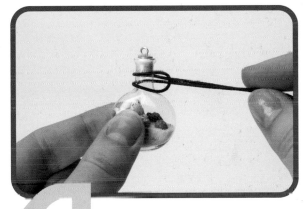

4 Use a larks head knot to tie an elastic or cord around the neck of the bottle (see page 16). Tie an extra knot in the cord or elastic for extra security.

Clear Geometric Jewelry

MATERIALS

- clear acrylic shapes (Heidi Grace Designs)
- paper pictures and images (photos copied onto paper or collage images, like those from The Vintage Workshop)
- decoupage glue
- paintbrush (for glue)
- pencil
- scissors
- jump rings
- jewelry chain or earring wires

Got homework coming out of your ears? Why not make earrings that say just that? Or how about showing your best bud how much you care by picturing your friendship on a pendant? With clear acrylic shapes you can transform any image you like into cool jewelry pieces.

Look for clear acrylic shapes, like the ones used for our sample project, in the scrapbook section of your local crafts store. Choose shapes with holes in the top for hanging.

Place the clear acrylic shape over your paper image to position the picture behind the shape. Use a pencil to trace around the outside of the shape and around the hole at the top. Cut out the hole following the traced line.

2 Brush decoupage glue in an even layer onto the back of the clear acrylic shape.

3 Using the traced lines as a guide, press the picture face-up onto the glued surface and smooth in place. The glue will look cloudy through the acrylic. Don't worry—it will dry clear. Let the piece dry.

4 With your scissors, trim off the paper around the edge of the acrylic shape.

5 Brush a coat of glue onto the back of the piece to seal the paper. Let the glue dry. Attach a jump ring through the hole at the top of the acrylic shape (see page 17). Hang the finished piece from a chain or earring wires. Or, instead of using a jump ring, you can simply thread cord through the hole.

Beaded Toe Rings

MATERIALS
- elastic jewelry cord (Stretch Magic)
- small beads
- white glue
- scissors

Fabulous tootsies deserve star treatment. Give your feet a treat with fun and fashionable beaded toe rings. These toe rings are fast to make and stretch to fit a variety of toe sizes. Perfect for the summer, these toe rings are great for showing off your favorite sandals or open-toe shoes.

Look for elastic jewelry cord in the jewelry-making section of your local crafts store or purchase some online. The elastic cord will stretch without cracking and the ends won't fray when cut. The cord comes in a variety of colors—there's even clear cord ideal for creating a "floating jewel" effect.

Thread a bead or beads onto the elastic. Tie a knot on both sides of the bead.

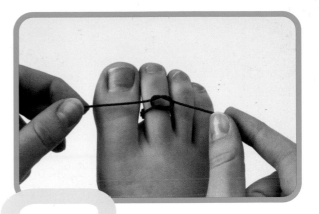

Tie the beaded elastic onto your toe to fit comfortably. Tie in a square knot, to hold securely.

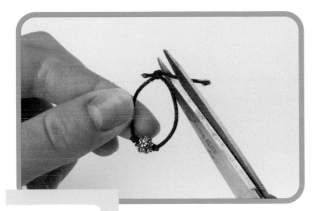

With your scissors, clip the ends of the elastic close to the knot.

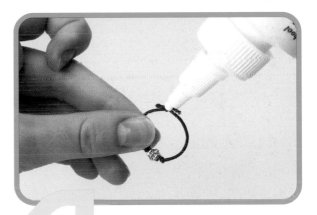

Add a dab of white glue or super glue to the knot to secure it in place.

Candy Wrapper Jewelry

Candy-wrapper jewelry is as much fun to make today as it was when your parents were kids. Save your bubblegum wrappers to make a retro-styled bracelet, or update the idea by making a pair of dangly earrings or an extra long candy-wrapper chain belt.

MATERIALS

- candy wrappers
- scissors
- gem or jewel glue
- for bracelet: hinged key ring (for closure)
- for earrings: 2 jump rings and 2 earring wires

Save lots of wrappers (gum wrappers are a good size). You will need about 15 wrappers to make a bracelet. Flatten and smooth the wrappers out. Cut the wrappers in half to make long rectangles.

Fold one of the cut rectangles in half lengthwise. Open the wrapper and fold each half to the middle, as shown (the fold line you made from folding the wrappers in half marks the middle).

With both sides remaining folded to the middle, fold the wrapper in half lengthwise again.

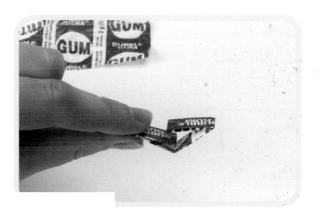

Fold the piece crosswise in half, matching the ends up, as shown.

Open this fold and fold each end in towards the middle. This will be your first link in the chain. Repeat steps 1 through 5 to make more links.

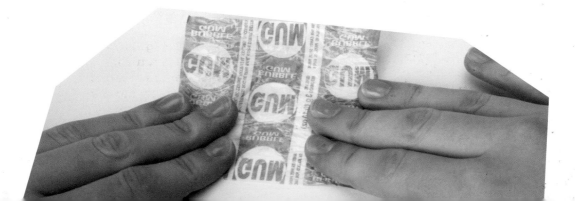

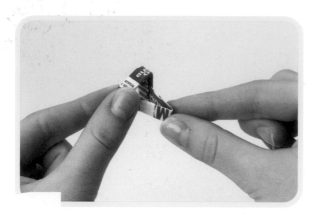

To link the folded wrappers together, slip the ends of one of the links through the open folds or "slits" in the other link, as shown.

Push one section all the way through to form an "L" shape with the wrappers. Continue in this manner adding a folded wrapper to the previous one to make a "chain" of wrappers.

When the chain of wrappers is long enough to fit around your wrist, glue the wrappers on each end of the chain closed. Apply the glue to the ends only, leaving an opening in the end wrapper for the closure. Let the glue dry.

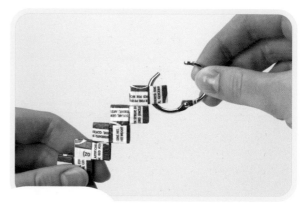

Slide a key ring through both ends of the chain and fasten the bracelet around your wrist.

If you don't have a key ring, you can use a piece of wire or a household twist-tie to hold the chain together. You can also slide the ends of the wrappers together as a chain, but they may slip out easily if they aren't secured with glue.

Pop Top Belt

MATERIALS
- soda can pop tops
- large safety pins

Don't throw that pop top away! Turn that so-called trash to treasure by fashioning the tops into a super cool belt. Silver looks great with blue jeans. For a heavy metal shine, make the belt extra long and wrap it around your waist several times.

Change the look of the belt by hanging beads or other small items from the safety pins. It's as easy as opening and closing the pins. Change the decorations to fit your mood or outfit.

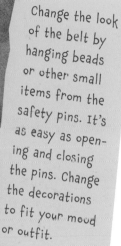

1 Collect the pop tops from your soda cans. Put the tops in a baggie or jar until you have enough to make a belt (about 25 pop tops should do it).

2 Open the safety pins to link the pop tops together into a chain. Start by hooking a safety pin through the bottom hole of your first pop top.

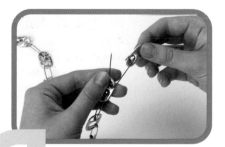

3 Slide the first pop top to the top of the pin and hook a second pop top onto the pin. Close the pin. Hook a second safety pin through the free hole of the second pop top and add a third pop top to that pin.

4 Continue in this manner linking the pop tops with safety pins, until you have a chain long enough to make a belt. (Make the chain a little longer if you want part of it to dangle from the end.) Use the safety pin you started with to fasten the belt around your waist.

FUN LOVIN'

Dog Tag Jean Charms

It's a dog's world! Stylish pooches have been wearing dangles for years. Now you can tap the trend by making your own charms from small metal dog tags. These dog tag charms can be hung from your jean loops or backpack. For a special surprise, use a charm as a gift tag. The charm will be a little extra gift in itself!

MATERIALS

- paper or fabric images (paper collage images by Teesha Moore, fabric by Michael Miller Fabrics)
- metal dog tag
- white glue
- paintbrush (for glue)
- pencil
- jump ring
- key chain or belt loop clip
- paper or fabric scissors
- small hole punch

1

Choose a paper or fabric image for the tag. Position the tag over the image and trace around the tag with a pencil. Mark the hole in the tag with your pencil. Cut out around the pencil line, trimming around the edges until the paper fits inside the tag.

2 At the spot where you marked the hole in the tag, punch a hole in the top of the paper, or cut a hole with your scissors if you are using fabric.

3 Brush white glue onto the tag. Press the image face up onto the tag over the glue. Let the glue dry.

4 If you want, seal the top of the image by brushing another layer of glue over the paper or fabric. Attach a jump ring to the top of the tag with pliers (see page 17), and hang the charm from a key chain or belt loop.

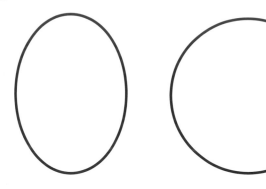

FABRIC
FLOWER
PETALS

BACK PIECE OF
FABRIC FLOWER

DUCT TAPE COIN PURSE

SHRINK PLASTIC
BUTTERFLY

Resources

Not sure where to find some of the materials listed? Below is a list of stores, outlets, and Web sites to help you get a hold of what you need. Most companies sell their products to retail and on-line stores. If your local craft and fabric store doesn't carry the item you need, you can contact the manufacturer to find the retailer nearest you that carries their products. You can also turn to the manufacturer for questions and tips on using their products.

DOVER PUBLICATIONS
store.doverpublications.com
Clip art books and CD-ROMs, copyright free illustrations

DUCK TAPE®
www.ducktapeclub.com
Duct tape and "skinny" duct tape, 20 colors

DUNCAN CRAFTS
www.duncancrafts.com
General craft supplies

JO-ANN FABRIC AND CRAFTS
www.joann.com
fabric, trims, and general craft supplies

GRAFIX®
19499 Miles Road
Cleveland, OH 44128
216-581-9050
www.graphixarts.com
Laminating Film®

7 GYPSIES
www.7gypsies.com
Scrapbook embellishments, little glass bottles

MICHAEL'S
www.michaels.com
General craft supplies

PLAID ENTERPRISES, INC.
3225 Westech Dr.
Norcross, GA 30092
1-800-842-4197
www.plaidonline.com
Mod Podge® decoupage glue

SCRAPWORKS
www.scrapworks.com
Scrapbook supplies, tie clips for ribbon

SHRINKY DINKS®
262-966-0305
262-966-0306 (fax)
www.shrinkydinks.com
Shrinkable plastic

THERM O WEB
www.thermoweb.com
PEELnSTICK™ Double Sided Adhesive Sheets or Tape

THE VINTAGE WORKSHOP
www.thevintageworkshop.com
Click-n-Craft CD-ROMs, downloadable art, inkjet printable fabrics, and papers

TEESHA MOORE
www.teeshamoore.com
Collage sheets, rubber stamps, and supplies

Index